Conquer™ the LPG Fitter Exam: Your Guide to Certification in Liquified Petroleum Gas Fitting

PHILIP MARTIN McCAULAY

Copyright © 2024 Philip Martin McCaulay
All rights reserved.
ISBN: 9798336375985
Imprint: Independently published

Table of Contents

Chapter 1: Introduction to Liquified Petroleum Gas (LPG) 1

Chapter 2: Safety Protocols and Best Practices 3

Chapter 3: LPG Codes, Regulations, and Compliance 6

Chapter 4: Tools and Equipment for LPG Fitting 9

Chapter 5: LPG Cylinder Installation and Handling 13

Chapter 6: Piping Systems for LPG 17

Chapter 7: Pressure Regulation and Metering Systems 21

Chapter 8: LPG Appliances: Installation and Maintenance 25

Chapter 9: Combustion Principles and Ventilation Requirements 29

Chapter 10: Leak Detection and Repair 33

Chapter 11: Testing and Commissioning LPG Systems 37

Chapter 12: Troubleshooting LPG Systems 41

Chapter 13: Advanced LPG Fitting Techniques 46

Chapter 14: Preparing for the LPG Fitter Exam 50

Chapter 15: Career Opportunities and Professional Development 55

Chapter 1: Introduction to Liquified Petroleum Gas (LPG)

Liquified Petroleum Gas, commonly referred to as LPG, is a versatile and widely used fuel source that plays a crucial role in various residential, commercial, and industrial applications. Understanding the fundamental properties and uses of LPG is essential for anyone pursuing a career as an LPG fitter. This chapter will introduce you to the basics of LPG, its applications, and the importance of certification in this specialized field.

LPG is a mixture of hydrocarbon gases, primarily propane and butane, which are stored in a liquid state under pressure. One of the key characteristics of LPG is its ability to vaporize easily at room temperature, making it an efficient and effective fuel source. When released from its pressurized container, LPG transforms into a gas that can be easily ignited and used for heating, cooking, and powering various appliances. This property makes LPG an ideal choice for locations where piped natural gas is not available or practical.

The versatility of LPG extends beyond its use in homes. In residential settings, LPG is commonly used for cooking, water heating, and space heating. It is particularly popular in rural and remote areas where natural gas infrastructure is lacking. In the commercial sector, LPG powers a wide range of equipment, from commercial kitchens and heating systems to industrial processes that require a reliable and controllable source of energy. Additionally, LPG is used in agriculture for crop drying, pest control, and greenhouse heating, showcasing its adaptability across various industries.

While LPG offers numerous benefits, it also presents specific challenges and risks. The pressurized nature of LPG storage requires careful handling, and its flammable properties necessitate strict adherence to safety protocols. As an LPG fitter, you will be responsible for ensuring that LPG systems are installed, maintained, and repaired according to the highest standards of safety and efficiency. This responsibility highlights the importance of obtaining proper certification in LPG fitting.

Certification in LPG fitting is more than just a credential; it is a testament to your knowledge, skills, and commitment to safety in this specialized field. The certification process involves rigorous training and testing to ensure that you are fully equipped to handle the complexities of working with LPG systems. From understanding the chemical properties of LPG to mastering the installation of gas piping and appliances, certification provides you with the expertise needed to perform your job safely and effectively.

Throughout this book, we will delve into the various aspects of LPG fitting, providing you with the knowledge and tools necessary to excel in your certification exam and your career. Each chapter will explore a different facet of LPG fitting, from safety protocols and regulatory compliance to advanced installation techniques and troubleshooting. By the end of this guide, you will have a comprehensive understanding of LPG systems and the confidence to pursue a successful career as a certified LPG fitter.

In the next chapter, we will focus on the critical topic of safety protocols and best practices for handling LPG. Safety is the cornerstone of all gas fitting work, and understanding how to manage the risks associated with LPG is essential for protecting yourself, your clients, and the community.

Chapter 2: Safety Protocols and Best Practices

Safety is the foundation of all work involving Liquified Petroleum Gas (LPG). As an LPG fitter, your primary responsibility is to ensure that every aspect of your work is conducted with the highest standards of safety in mind. This chapter delves into the essential safety protocols and best practices that you must adhere to when handling and installing LPG systems. Understanding these principles not only protects you and your clients but also ensures that you are in compliance with industry regulations and standards.

LPG is a highly flammable substance, and its safe handling requires a thorough understanding of its properties. One of the key safety considerations is the storage of LPG. LPG is stored under pressure in liquid form, which means that any breach of the container can result in a rapid release of gas, posing a significant fire hazard. Therefore, it is crucial to store LPG cylinders in a well-ventilated area, away from sources of heat or open flames. The storage area should also be secured to prevent unauthorized access and protected from physical damage that could compromise the integrity of the cylinders.

When handling LPG cylinders, always ensure that you are using the appropriate personal protective equipment, or PPE. This includes gloves to protect your hands from cold burns caused by the rapid expansion of gas, safety glasses to shield your eyes from potential splashes of liquid gas, and flame-resistant clothing to reduce the risk of injury in the event of a fire. It is also important to have a fire extinguisher rated for gas fires readily available at all times when working with LPG.

The transportation of LPG cylinders requires careful planning and execution. Cylinders should be transported in an upright position to prevent the liquid gas from escaping through the valve. If possible, secure the cylinders in a well-ventilated compartment, separate from the driver's area, to reduce the risk of exposure to any leaking gas. During transportation, it is essential to avoid rough handling or dropping the cylinders, as this could damage the valve or cylinder, leading to a dangerous situation.

During the installation process, one of the most critical safety practices is to thoroughly inspect all equipment and materials before use. This includes checking the LPG cylinders, regulators, hoses, and fittings for any signs of damage or wear. Even a small defect can lead to a significant safety hazard, so it is essential to replace any damaged components before proceeding with the installation. Additionally, all connections must be properly secured and leak-tested before the system is put into operation.

Leak detection is a vital aspect of ensuring the safety of an LPG system. A gas leak, even a small one, can quickly escalate into a dangerous situation if not addressed promptly. To detect leaks, apply a soapy water solution to all connections and watch for the formation of bubbles, which indicate the presence of gas escaping from the system. If a leak is detected, immediately shut off the gas supply and repair the leak before proceeding. It is also important to educate your clients on how to recognize the signs of a gas leak, such as the distinct smell of LPG or the hissing sound of escaping gas, and what steps they should take if they suspect a leak.

In addition to leak detection, proper ventilation is essential in any area where LPG is used. Since LPG is heavier than air, it tends to settle in low areas, which can create a hazardous accumulation of gas if not properly ventilated. Ensure that all installations include adequate ventilation to disperse any gas that may escape, reducing the risk of fire or explosion.

Emergency preparedness is another crucial element of LPG safety. As an LPG fitter, you must be prepared to respond quickly and effectively in the event of an emergency. This includes knowing the location of emergency shut-off valves, understanding how to safely evacuate the area, and being familiar with the proper use of fire extinguishers and other emergency equipment. Regularly review and practice emergency procedures to ensure that you can act swiftly in a crisis.

Finally, it is important to stay informed about the latest safety standards and best practices in the LPG industry. Safety regulations are continually evolving, and staying up-to-date with these changes is essential for maintaining a safe working environment. Participate in ongoing training and certification programs, and regularly review industry publications and guidelines to ensure that your knowledge remains current.

In summary, safety is the most critical aspect of your work as an LPG fitter. By adhering to the safety protocols and best practices outlined in this chapter, you can protect yourself, your clients, and the community from the risks associated with LPG. Remember that safety is not just a set of rules to follow, but a mindset that should guide every decision you make in your work.

In the next chapter, we will explore the codes, regulations, and compliance requirements that govern the installation and maintenance of LPG systems. Understanding these regulations is essential for ensuring that your work meets all legal and safety standards.

Chapter 3: LPG Codes, Regulations, and Compliance

Understanding and adhering to the codes, regulations, and compliance requirements that govern LPG fitting is critical to ensuring both safety and legality in your work. As an LPG fitter, you must be well-versed in the various laws and standards that apply to the installation, maintenance, and operation of LPG systems. This chapter will guide you through the essential regulatory frameworks and the importance of compliance in the LPG industry.

The regulatory landscape for LPG fitting is complex, as it involves both national and local codes. These regulations are designed to protect public safety by ensuring that all LPG systems are installed and maintained according to strict standards. Failure to comply with these regulations can result in serious consequences, including fines, legal action, and, most importantly, safety hazards that could endanger lives.

At the national level, one of the primary standards governing LPG fitting is set by organizations such as the National Fire Protection Association (NFPA) in the United States. The NFPA 58: Liquefied Petroleum Gas Code is a key document that outlines the requirements for the safe storage, handling, transportation, and use of LPG. This code covers a wide range of topics, including the design and construction of LPG containers, installation requirements, and safety procedures. As an LPG fitter, you must be familiar with NFPA 58 and ensure that all your work complies with its guidelines.

In addition to national standards like NFPA 58, you must also adhere to local building codes and regulations. These codes can vary significantly from one jurisdiction to another, so it is important to understand the specific requirements that apply in the area where you are working. Local codes may dictate additional safety measures, such as specific installation practices, zoning restrictions, or environmental considerations. Before starting any project, it is essential to review the local codes and obtain any necessary permits or approvals.

Compliance with these regulations is not just about following the law; it is about ensuring that every LPG system you work on is safe and reliable. This begins with proper planning and design. Before installing an LPG system, you must conduct a thorough site assessment to identify any potential hazards and determine the best location for the equipment. This includes considering factors such as ventilation, proximity to ignition sources, and access for maintenance. By addressing these issues during the planning stage, you can avoid many common safety problems and ensure that the installation meets all regulatory requirements.

During the installation process, it is essential to follow all prescribed procedures and use materials that comply with the relevant standards. This includes selecting the correct type of piping, valves, and regulators, as well as ensuring that all connections are properly secured and leak-tested. Adhering to these standards not only ensures the safety of the system but also helps to prevent costly repairs or modifications down the line.

Once the installation is complete, proper documentation is crucial for demonstrating compliance. This includes keeping detailed records of the installation process, including the materials used, the results of safety tests, and any inspections or approvals obtained from local authorities. Maintaining accurate records is important not only for legal purposes but also for ensuring that the system can be properly maintained and serviced in the future.

Regular inspections and maintenance are also essential components of compliance. Many jurisdictions require periodic inspections of LPG systems to ensure that they remain in good working order and continue to meet safety standards. As an LPG fitter, you must be prepared to conduct these inspections and address any issues that may arise. This includes checking for leaks, testing safety devices, and verifying that all components are functioning correctly. By staying on top of maintenance and inspections, you can prevent minor problems from becoming major safety hazards.

In addition to adhering to codes and regulations, it is important to stay informed about any changes or updates to the standards that govern LPG fitting. The regulatory landscape is constantly evolving, and new technologies, materials, and practices are regularly introduced. To stay compliant, you must engage in ongoing professional development, including attending training sessions, reading industry publications, and participating in certification programs. By staying current with the latest developments in the industry, you can ensure that your work continues to meet the highest standards of safety and quality.

In conclusion, understanding and complying with the codes, regulations, and compliance requirements that govern LPG fitting is essential for protecting public safety and ensuring the legality of your work. By familiarizing yourself with national standards like NFPA 58, adhering to local building codes, and maintaining proper documentation, you can ensure that every LPG system you install is safe, reliable, and fully compliant with all applicable regulations.

In the next chapter, we will discuss the tools and equipment essential for LPG fitting, providing detailed insights into how to select, use, and maintain the tools of your trade.

Chapter 4: Tools and Equipment for LPG Fitting

As an LPG fitter, having the right tools and equipment is essential for performing your job safely, efficiently, and to the highest standards. Each tool has a specific role in the installation, maintenance, and repair of LPG systems, and knowing how to use them correctly is crucial for achieving successful outcomes. In this chapter, we will explore the various tools and equipment you will need as an LPG fitter, as well as best practices for their selection, use, and maintenance.

One of the most fundamental tools in any LPG fitter's arsenal is the **pipe wrench**. Pipe wrenches are essential for gripping and turning pipes and fittings, and they come in various sizes to accommodate different diameters of pipe. When selecting a pipe wrench, it's important to choose one that is the right size for the job at hand. Using a wrench that is too large can damage the pipe, while a wrench that is too small may not provide enough leverage. Additionally, always ensure that the teeth of the wrench are in good condition, as worn teeth can slip and cause injury or damage to the pipe.

Another critical tool is the **adjustable wrench**, often used for tightening or loosening nuts and bolts on fittings, regulators, and appliances. The adjustable wrench is versatile, allowing you to work with different sizes of fasteners without needing a separate tool for each size. However, it's important to ensure that the jaws of the wrench are properly adjusted and securely grip the fastener to avoid slippage, which could lead to injury or damage to the equipment.

For cutting pipes to the correct length, a **pipe cutter** is indispensable. Pipe cutters are designed to make clean, precise cuts in various types of piping materials, including copper, steel, and plastic. Unlike saws, which can leave rough edges and burrs, a pipe cutter provides a smooth, even cut that ensures a proper fit and seal when joining pipes. When using a pipe cutter, it's important to rotate the tool evenly around the pipe, applying consistent pressure to avoid uneven cuts.

When working with flexible gas hoses, a **hose cutter** is the tool of choice. Hose cutters are specifically designed to cut through the tough, reinforced materials used in gas hoses, providing a clean cut without crushing or deforming the hose. This is important for ensuring that the hose fits securely onto fittings and that there are no leaks. As with pipe cutters, using a hose cutter requires a steady hand and even pressure to achieve the best results.

A **tubing bender** is another essential tool, particularly when working with copper or other soft metal piping. Tubing benders allow you to create precise bends in the pipe without kinking or weakening it. This is important for maintaining the integrity of the piping system and ensuring a smooth flow of gas. When using a tubing bender, it's important to measure and mark the pipe carefully before bending to ensure that the bends are in the correct location and at the proper angle.

For joining pipes, a **pipe threader** is often necessary, especially when working with threaded steel or iron pipes. Pipe threaders cut threads onto the ends of pipes, allowing them to be screwed into fittings or other pipes. Proper threading is crucial for creating a tight, leak-proof seal. When threading pipes, it's important to use the correct size die for the pipe and to apply a consistent amount of pressure to ensure even, accurate threads.

In addition to these basic tools, there are several specialized tools that you may need for specific tasks in LPG fitting. For example, a **manometer** is used to measure gas pressure in the system, ensuring that it is within safe and appropriate levels. A **gas leak detector** is essential for identifying even the smallest leaks in the system, helping to prevent potential safety hazards. **Torque wrenches** are used to apply a specific amount of force to fasteners, ensuring that they are tightened to the manufacturer's specifications without over-tightening, which could damage the components.

In terms of equipment, one of the most important items is the **pressure regulator**. The pressure regulator is a critical component of any LPG system, as it controls the flow of gas from the cylinder to the appliances. Selecting the right pressure regulator for the specific application is essential for ensuring the safe and efficient operation of the system. When installing a pressure regulator, it's important to follow the manufacturer's instructions carefully, ensuring that all connections are secure and that the regulator is properly calibrated.

Another key piece of equipment is the **flame arrestor**, which is used to prevent flames from traveling back into the gas supply line, a potentially dangerous situation. Flame arrestors are typically installed in line with the gas piping and require regular inspection and maintenance to ensure they are functioning correctly.

Safety equipment is also an integral part of your toolkit as an LPG fitter. This includes personal protective equipment (PPE) such as gloves, safety glasses, and flame-resistant clothing, which are essential for protecting yourself from the hazards associated with working with LPG. Additionally, having a fire extinguisher rated for gas fires on hand is crucial for dealing with any emergencies that may arise during your work.

Proper maintenance of your tools and equipment is vital for ensuring their longevity and effectiveness. Regularly inspect your tools for signs of wear or damage, and replace any that are no longer in good working condition. Keeping your tools clean and properly stored will also help to extend their lifespan and ensure that they are ready for use when needed.

In conclusion, having the right tools and equipment is essential for performing your job as an LPG fitter safely and effectively. By selecting the appropriate tools for each task, using them correctly, and maintaining them properly, you can ensure that your work is of the highest quality and that you are able to complete your tasks efficiently and safely.

In the next chapter, we will discuss the specific techniques and considerations involved in the installation and handling of LPG cylinders. Proper installation is crucial for ensuring the safe operation of LPG systems, and this chapter will provide detailed guidance on how to achieve this.

Chapter 5: LPG Cylinder Installation and Handling

The installation and handling of LPG cylinders are among the most critical tasks an LPG fitter will perform. Given the pressurized nature of these cylinders and the flammable gas they contain, it is essential to follow strict procedures to ensure safety at all times. This chapter will guide you through the key techniques and considerations for the safe and effective installation and handling of LPG cylinders.

LPG cylinders are typically stored and transported in a liquid state under pressure. When released, the liquid rapidly vaporizes into gas, making it highly flammable. Because of this, the first and foremost consideration when working with LPG cylinders is safety. The proper handling of these cylinders begins with understanding their basic characteristics, including the pressure they are under and the potential hazards they present if mishandled.

When receiving an LPG cylinder, the first step is to inspect it for any signs of damage or wear. Look for dents, rust, or other physical damage that could compromise the integrity of the cylinder. Check the valve to ensure it is in good condition and that there are no leaks. If you detect any issues, do not proceed with the installation; instead, return the cylinder to the supplier and request a replacement. It's crucial that you only work with cylinders that are in perfect condition to prevent any accidents.

The next step in the installation process is positioning the cylinder correctly. LPG cylinders must always be stored and used in an upright position. This ensures that the liquid gas inside remains at the bottom of the cylinder while the vaporized gas collects at the top, where it can be safely drawn off through the valve. Never lay a cylinder on its side, as this could cause liquid gas to enter the regulator and piping, leading to potentially dangerous situations.

Choosing the right location for the cylinder is also vital. Cylinders should be placed in a well-ventilated area to prevent the accumulation of gas in the event of a leak. They should be kept away from sources of heat, sparks, or open flames, as LPG is highly flammable. Additionally, ensure that the cylinder is stored in a secure area where it will not be knocked over or damaged. If you are installing the cylinder outdoors, make sure it is protected from the elements and that the location complies with any local regulations regarding LPG storage.

Once the cylinder is in position, you can proceed with the connection process. Start by attaching the regulator to the cylinder valve. The regulator is a critical component that controls the pressure of the gas as it exits the cylinder and enters the system. Before connecting the regulator, make sure the valve is fully closed to prevent gas from escaping. When attaching the regulator, ensure that the connection is secure and that there are no gaps or loose fittings. After the regulator is in place, you can attach the hose that will carry the gas to the appliances.

After connecting the regulator and hose, it is essential to perform a leak test before turning on the gas. Leak testing is a simple but crucial step in the installation process. To test for leaks, apply a soapy water solution to all connections, including the valve, regulator, and hose fittings. If you see any bubbles forming, this indicates a leak. In the event of a leak, immediately shut off the valve and recheck all connections. Do not proceed with the installation until the leak has been fixed and you have verified that the system is secure.

Once you have confirmed that there are no leaks, you can slowly open the cylinder valve to allow gas to flow into the system. Always open the valve slowly to prevent a sudden rush of gas, which could cause pressure surges or trigger safety devices in the system. As the gas begins to flow, listen for any unusual noises and check the pressure gauge on the regulator to ensure that the pressure is within the safe operating range.

After the system is pressurized, conduct a final inspection to ensure that everything is functioning correctly. Check that the gas is reaching the appliances and that they are operating as expected. If you encounter any issues, such as appliances not igniting or irregular flame patterns, shut off the gas supply and troubleshoot the problem before proceeding.

In addition to proper installation, it's important to handle LPG cylinders with care during transportation and storage. When transporting cylinders, always secure them in an upright position to prevent tipping or rolling. Cylinders should never be transported in the passenger compartment of a vehicle, as any gas that escapes could create a hazardous situation. Instead, place them in a well-ventilated area, such as the bed of a truck, and secure them to prevent movement.

When storing LPG cylinders, follow the same guidelines as for installation: keep them upright, in a well-ventilated area, and away from sources of heat or ignition. Never store cylinders in confined spaces or indoors unless specifically designed for that purpose. If you are storing multiple cylinders, ensure that they are spaced apart to allow for proper ventilation and easy access in case of an emergency.

Handling empty cylinders requires just as much care as handling full ones. Even when a cylinder appears empty, it may still contain residual gas that can pose a risk. Treat empty cylinders with the same precautions as full ones, and ensure that the valve is securely closed. Mark empty cylinders clearly to avoid confusion, and store them separately from full cylinders.

In conclusion, the safe installation and handling of LPG cylinders are critical to preventing accidents and ensuring the reliable operation of LPG systems. By following the procedures outlined in this chapter, you can minimize the risks associated with LPG and ensure that your installations are safe and compliant with all relevant regulations.

In the next chapter, we will explore the piping systems used in LPG installations, including materials, sizing, and installation techniques. Properly installed piping is essential for the safe and efficient delivery of LPG, and this chapter will provide detailed guidance on how to achieve this.

Chapter 6: Piping Systems for LPG

Piping systems are the backbone of any LPG installation, serving as the conduit through which the gas travels from the storage cylinder to the various appliances. The integrity and proper installation of these pipes are critical to the safe and efficient operation of the entire system. In this chapter, we will delve into the different types of materials used in LPG piping, the importance of proper sizing, and the techniques for installing and maintaining these systems.

The first consideration in LPG piping is the selection of the appropriate material. The materials used for LPG piping must be able to withstand the pressures involved, resist corrosion, and be compatible with LPG. Common materials include copper, steel, and polyethylene, each of which has its own advantages and applications.

Copper is a popular choice for LPG piping due to its durability, flexibility, and resistance to corrosion. It is particularly well-suited for residential installations where pipes need to be routed through tight spaces or around obstacles. Copper pipes can be easily bent and shaped, which allows for a more straightforward installation process in complex layouts. However, copper should not be used in direct contact with concrete or other corrosive materials unless properly insulated.

Steel piping, particularly black iron or galvanized steel, is another common choice, especially in commercial and industrial settings. Steel is extremely strong and can handle higher pressures than copper, making it ideal for larger installations that require long runs of piping or where the gas pressure is higher. Steel pipes are typically used above ground and in areas where they are less likely to be exposed to moisture, as steel can corrode if not properly protected.

Polyethylene (PE) piping is often used for underground LPG installations. PE pipes are lightweight, flexible, and resistant to both corrosion and environmental factors, making them an excellent choice for buried lines. These pipes are usually laid in a trench and must be protected from physical damage during installation. It's important to ensure that PE pipes are correctly joined using specialized fittings and techniques to prevent leaks and ensure the integrity of the system.

Once the material has been selected, the next crucial step is determining the correct size for the piping. Proper sizing is essential for ensuring that the gas pressure remains within safe and effective limits as it travels through the system. If the pipes are too small, they may restrict the flow of gas, leading to pressure drops that can cause appliances to malfunction. On the other hand, pipes that are too large can be unnecessarily expensive and difficult to install.

To size the piping correctly, you need to consider several factors, including the distance the gas must travel, the pressure at the source, and the demand of the appliances connected to the system. The longer the pipe run, the more pressure is lost due to friction, so longer runs may require larger diameter pipes. Additionally, the total BTU (British Thermal Unit) load of all connected appliances must be calculated to determine the appropriate pipe size. This calculation ensures that each appliance receives the necessary amount of gas to function correctly.

Once the material and size have been determined, the installation process can begin. Proper installation is key to the safety and efficiency of the LPG system. The first step is to carefully plan the layout of the piping, taking into account the location of the LPG cylinder, the appliances, and any obstacles or hazards that might affect the installation. Pipes should be routed in a way that minimizes the number of bends and fittings, as each bend or fitting can increase the potential for leaks and reduce gas flow.

When installing the pipes, it's important to follow the manufacturer's guidelines and industry best practices. For example, when using copper pipes, ensure that the bends are made using a proper tubing bender to avoid kinking the pipe, which can weaken it and restrict gas flow. For steel pipes, ensure that all threads are cut cleanly and that thread sealant is applied to ensure a gas-tight connection.

The connections between pipes and fittings must be secure to prevent leaks. This typically involves the use of threaded fittings, which should be tightened to the manufacturer's specifications. Over-tightening can damage the threads and lead to leaks, while under-tightening may result in a poor seal. It's also important to check that all fittings are compatible with the type of gas being used and that they meet the necessary standards for LPG installations.

After the pipes have been installed and all connections made, the entire system must be pressure-tested to ensure there are no leaks. This involves sealing the system and applying pressure using a manometer or similar device. The pressure is then monitored for a set period to ensure that it remains stable, indicating that the system is gas-tight. If any pressure drop is detected, the source of the leak must be identified and repaired before the system can be put into service.

In addition to installation, regular maintenance of the piping system is essential for ensuring its long-term reliability and safety. This includes periodic inspections to check for signs of wear, corrosion, or damage, particularly at joints and fittings where leaks are more likely to occur. Any issues that are identified should be addressed immediately to prevent potential safety hazards. It's also important to ensure that any repairs or modifications to the system are carried out by qualified personnel following the same standards and procedures as the original installation.

In conclusion, the selection, sizing, and installation of LPG piping are critical aspects of creating a safe and efficient LPG system. By understanding the properties of different materials, calculating the correct pipe size, and following best practices for installation and maintenance, you can ensure that the system operates smoothly and safely for years to come.

In the next chapter, we will discuss the role of pressure regulation and metering systems in LPG installations. These components are essential for controlling the flow of gas and ensuring that the system operates within safe parameters.

Chapter 7: Pressure Regulation and Metering Systems

In any LPG system, the role of pressure regulation and metering systems is crucial. These components ensure that the gas is delivered at the correct pressure and in the right quantities, making them essential for the safe and efficient operation of the system. This chapter will explore how pressure regulators and meters function, the different types available, and best practices for their installation and maintenance.

At the heart of every LPG system is the **pressure regulator**. The primary function of the pressure regulator is to control the flow of gas from the high-pressure storage cylinder to the lower-pressure piping system and appliances. LPG is stored in a liquid state under high pressure, typically between 100 and 200 pounds per square inch (psi), depending on the ambient temperature. However, most appliances are designed to operate at much lower pressures, usually between 6 and 11 inches of water column, which is approximately 0.22 to 0.40 psi. The regulator reduces the high pressure from the cylinder to a level that is safe for the appliances to use.

There are several types of pressure regulators used in LPG systems, each designed for specific applications. The most common type is the **single-stage regulator**, which reduces the cylinder pressure to the desired outlet pressure in one step. Single-stage regulators are simple and cost-effective, making them ideal for small residential installations where the distance between the cylinder and the appliances is relatively short. However, because the outlet pressure can vary with changes in the cylinder pressure, single-stage regulators may not be suitable for installations with long pipe runs or where precise pressure control is required.

For more complex installations, a **two-stage regulator** is often used. In a two-stage system, the first stage reduces the cylinder pressure to an intermediate level, typically around 10 to 20 psi. The second stage then further reduces this pressure to the final outlet pressure required by the appliances. Two-stage regulators provide more stable and consistent pressure control, making them suitable for larger residential, commercial, or industrial installations where precise pressure regulation is critical. They are also better equipped to handle variations in cylinder pressure due to temperature changes or fluctuations in gas demand.

In addition to standard regulators, there are **automatic changeover regulators** designed for systems with multiple cylinders. These regulators automatically switch the gas supply from an empty cylinder to a full one, ensuring a continuous flow of gas without interruption. Changeover regulators are commonly used in commercial or industrial settings where maintaining a constant gas supply is essential. They also provide an added layer of convenience and safety, as the user does not need to manually switch cylinders when one is depleted.

Proper installation of the pressure regulator is vital for ensuring the safety and efficiency of the LPG system. The regulator should be installed as close to the cylinder as possible, in an upright position, and in a location that is protected from physical damage and environmental factors such as extreme heat, moisture, or direct sunlight. The inlet connection of the regulator must be securely attached to the cylinder valve, using the correct type of fitting and ensuring that there are no leaks. It's important to use a wrench to tighten the connection, but care should be taken not to over-tighten, as this could damage the threads or the regulator.

After the regulator is installed, it's essential to check the system for leaks using a soapy water solution, as described in previous chapters. The outlet pressure should also be tested to ensure that it falls within the desired range for the appliances connected to the system. If the pressure is too high or too low, adjustments may need to be made to the regulator, or the regulator may need to be replaced with a different type that is better suited to the specific installation.

Another critical component of an LPG system is the **metering device**. The meter measures the amount of gas flowing through the system, providing a way to monitor gas usage and detect potential issues such as leaks or excessive consumption. In residential installations, meters are often used by gas suppliers to track usage for billing purposes. In commercial or industrial settings, meters are used to monitor gas consumption as part of energy management and safety programs.

There are several types of gas meters, including **diaphragm meters**, **rotary meters**, and **turbine meters**, each of which operates on a different principle. Diaphragm meters are the most common type used in residential installations. They measure gas flow by counting the number of times a flexible diaphragm moves as gas passes through the meter. Rotary meters are used in commercial and industrial settings where higher flow rates are encountered. They operate by measuring the rotation of two interlocking rotors as gas flows through the meter. Turbine meters, also used in high-flow applications, measure gas flow by detecting the speed at which a turbine spins in response to the gas passing through it.

The installation of gas meters should follow the manufacturer's guidelines and local regulations. Meters should be installed in a location that is easily accessible for reading and maintenance, and they should be protected from damage and environmental factors. It's important to ensure that the meter is correctly calibrated and that all connections are secure and leak-free.

Regular maintenance of pressure regulators and meters is essential for ensuring the ongoing safety and efficiency of the LPG system. Regulators should be inspected periodically for signs of wear, corrosion, or damage. The diaphragm or other internal components may degrade over time, affecting the regulator's ability to maintain consistent pressure. If any issues are detected, the regulator should be replaced to prevent potential safety hazards.

Similarly, gas meters should be checked regularly to ensure they are functioning correctly and providing accurate readings. Inaccurate meters can lead to incorrect billing or failure to detect issues such as leaks or excessive usage. If a meter is found to be faulty, it should be recalibrated or replaced as needed.

In summary, pressure regulation and metering systems are critical components of any LPG installation. By understanding how these systems work, selecting the appropriate type for your specific application, and following best practices for installation and maintenance, you can ensure that the LPG system operates safely and efficiently.

In the next chapter, we will explore the installation and maintenance of LPG appliances, providing detailed guidance on how to safely connect and service a range of gas-powered devices.

Chapter 8: LPG Appliances: Installation and Maintenance

LPG appliances are central to the functionality of any LPG system, serving various purposes from heating and cooking to powering industrial equipment. Ensuring the safe and efficient installation and maintenance of these appliances is crucial for the overall performance of the system. In this chapter, we will explore the best practices for installing and maintaining a range of LPG-powered appliances, along with the specific safety considerations that must be taken into account.

The first step in installing an LPG appliance is selecting the appropriate model for the specific application. LPG appliances come in a variety of types, including water heaters, stoves, furnaces, and industrial burners. Each appliance is designed to operate within certain parameters, such as gas pressure and flow rate, which must be compatible with the LPG system you have installed. It is important to consult the manufacturer's specifications to ensure that the appliance will function correctly with the existing gas supply.

Before beginning the installation, it is essential to review the appliance's installation manual thoroughly. This manual provides detailed instructions on how to connect the appliance to the gas supply, venting requirements, and safety precautions. Following these instructions closely is critical to ensuring the appliance operates safely and efficiently. Additionally, you should familiarize yourself with any local codes or regulations that apply to the installation of LPG appliances, as these may dictate specific requirements beyond those provided by the manufacturer.

When installing an LPG appliance, the first step is to position it correctly. The appliance should be placed in a location that allows for adequate ventilation and easy access for maintenance. For example, gas stoves should be installed in a well-ventilated kitchen area, away from flammable materials, while water heaters should be located near the points of use to minimize heat loss through the pipes. It is also important to ensure that there is sufficient clearance around the appliance to prevent overheating and allow for the safe dissipation of heat.

The next step is connecting the appliance to the gas supply. This involves attaching the gas line to the appliance's inlet connection using the appropriate fittings and ensuring a secure, leak-free connection. Depending on the type of appliance and the installation, you may need to use flexible gas connectors, which allow for easier alignment and adjustment of the appliance. These connectors must be properly rated for LPG and installed according to the manufacturer's guidelines to prevent leaks.

After connecting the gas line, it is crucial to perform a leak test before operating the appliance. This can be done by applying a soapy water solution to all connections and watching for bubbles, which indicate a leak. If a leak is detected, immediately shut off the gas supply and tighten or re-secure the connections until the leak is eliminated. Only after confirming that there are no leaks should you proceed with igniting the appliance.

Proper venting is another critical aspect of LPG appliance installation. Many LPG appliances, particularly those used for heating, produce combustion byproducts that must be safely vented to the outside. These byproducts can include carbon monoxide, which is highly toxic and can be fatal if it accumulates in an enclosed space. The venting system should be installed according to the manufacturer's instructions and local codes, ensuring that it is properly sized and free from obstructions. Regular inspection and maintenance of the venting system are essential to ensure that it remains effective and safe.

Once the appliance is installed and connected, the final step is to test its operation. Turn on the appliance and monitor its performance, checking for proper ignition, flame stability, and even heat distribution. The flame should be a steady blue, indicating complete combustion. If the flame is yellow or flickering, this could indicate incomplete combustion, which may be caused by issues such as insufficient air supply or incorrect gas pressure. In such cases, it is important to troubleshoot and resolve the problem before allowing the appliance to be used regularly.

Routine maintenance is essential for keeping LPG appliances in good working order and ensuring their longevity. Maintenance tasks vary depending on the type of appliance but generally include cleaning burners, inspecting and replacing worn components, and checking the venting system for blockages or damage. For example, in gas stoves, it is important to clean the burners regularly to prevent the buildup of food debris or grease, which can obstruct gas flow and lead to uneven heating or ignition problems. Similarly, in water heaters, it is important to periodically check the burner assembly and pilot light, as well as flush the tank to remove sediment that can reduce efficiency and cause damage.

It is also important to regularly check the appliance's safety devices, such as thermocouples and flame sensors, which are designed to shut off the gas supply if a problem is detected. These components play a crucial role in preventing accidents and ensuring the safe operation of the appliance. If any of these devices show signs of wear or malfunction, they should be replaced immediately.

In addition to regular maintenance, LPG appliances should be inspected annually by a qualified technician. This inspection should include a thorough examination of the gas connections, venting system, and all components of the appliance to ensure they are in good condition and functioning correctly. Annual inspections are also an opportunity to identify and address any potential issues before they develop into more serious problems.

In conclusion, the installation and maintenance of LPG appliances are critical to the safety and efficiency of the entire LPG system. By following the manufacturer's instructions, adhering to local codes and regulations, and performing regular maintenance and inspections, you can ensure that the appliances operate safely and effectively, providing reliable service for years to come.

In the next chapter, we will explore the principles of combustion and the importance of proper ventilation in LPG systems. Understanding these concepts is essential for ensuring that LPG appliances operate safely and efficiently.

Chapter 9: Combustion Principles and Ventilation Requirements

Combustion is the process that powers most LPG appliances, whether they are used for heating, cooking, or industrial applications. Understanding the principles of combustion and the importance of proper ventilation is crucial for ensuring the safe and efficient operation of these appliances. In this chapter, we will delve into the science of combustion, the factors that influence it, and the ventilation requirements necessary to maintain a safe environment.

At its core, combustion is a chemical reaction between a fuel and an oxidizer, typically oxygen, that produces heat and light. In the case of LPG, the fuel consists primarily of propane and butane, which are hydrocarbons. When these gases mix with oxygen in the right proportions and are ignited, they burn, releasing energy in the form of heat. The products of complete combustion are carbon dioxide, water vapor, and heat. This is the ideal scenario, as complete combustion ensures that the fuel is used efficiently and that harmful byproducts are minimized.

For combustion to occur, three elements must be present: fuel, oxygen, and an ignition source. This is often referred to as the "fire triangle." Removing any one of these elements will prevent combustion, which is why safety measures such as shutting off the gas supply or ventilating a space are effective in preventing fires or explosions. In the context of LPG appliances, ensuring the correct balance of fuel and oxygen is key to achieving efficient combustion.

The ratio of fuel to oxygen is known as the air-to-fuel ratio, and it plays a critical role in determining the efficiency of combustion. If there is too little oxygen, the combustion process becomes incomplete, leading to the production of carbon monoxide, a dangerous and potentially lethal gas. Incomplete combustion also results in the formation of soot and other unburned hydrocarbons, which can clog burners and reduce the efficiency of the appliance. On the other hand, if there is too much oxygen, the combustion process can be less efficient, as excess air can cool the flame and reduce the amount of heat produced.

To achieve complete combustion, it is essential to provide the right amount of ventilation. Ventilation ensures that there is a sufficient supply of fresh air to mix with the LPG before it is ignited. In enclosed spaces, particularly those that are airtight or poorly ventilated, the oxygen levels can drop, leading to incomplete combustion and the buildup of harmful gases. This is why it is crucial to follow the manufacturer's recommendations for ventilation when installing LPG appliances.

There are two primary types of ventilation that must be considered: combustion air and exhaust ventilation. **Combustion air** refers to the air that is required to support the combustion process. This air must be supplied directly to the appliance, either from the room in which it is located or from an external source. The amount of combustion air required depends on the size and type of the appliance, as well as the specific installation conditions. For example, larger appliances or those with higher heat output will require more combustion air than smaller units.

Exhaust ventilation is equally important, as it is responsible for removing the products of combustion from the appliance and venting them safely outside the building. Proper exhaust ventilation ensures that harmful gases such as carbon monoxide are not allowed to accumulate in the living space. Exhaust systems must be correctly sized and installed to match the requirements of the appliance. This includes ensuring that the exhaust vent is properly sealed, free from obstructions, and terminates in a location where the gases can disperse safely.

In some installations, particularly those involving sealed combustion appliances, a **balanced ventilation system** may be used. Sealed combustion appliances draw combustion air from outside the building and exhaust the combustion products directly outside, without affecting the indoor air quality. These systems are particularly advantageous in energy-efficient buildings where minimizing air leakage is important. However, they require careful installation and maintenance to ensure that the air supply and exhaust systems remain balanced and function correctly.

One of the key indicators of proper combustion is the appearance of the flame. In an LPG appliance, a **blue flame** is a sign of complete combustion, indicating that the air-to-fuel ratio is correct and that the appliance is operating efficiently. A yellow or orange flame, on the other hand, indicates incomplete combustion, which may be caused by a lack of oxygen, incorrect burner settings, or clogged burners. If you observe a yellow or orange flame, it is important to troubleshoot the issue immediately, as this can be a sign of dangerous conditions such as carbon monoxide production.

In addition to proper ventilation, regular maintenance of the appliance's burners and combustion system is essential for ensuring efficient combustion. Burners should be cleaned periodically to remove any soot or debris that may have accumulated, as this can obstruct the flow of gas and air and lead to incomplete combustion. The burner settings should also be checked to ensure that they are properly adjusted for the type of gas being used and the specific installation conditions.

Finally, it is important to educate your clients on the importance of proper ventilation and the signs of incomplete combustion. They should be made aware of the dangers of carbon monoxide and instructed on how to use their appliances safely. Installing carbon monoxide detectors in areas where LPG appliances are used is a crucial safety measure, as these devices can provide an early warning if dangerous levels of the gas are detected.

In conclusion, understanding the principles of combustion and the importance of proper ventilation is essential for ensuring the safe and efficient operation of LPG appliances. By providing the correct air-to-fuel ratio, ensuring adequate ventilation, and maintaining the appliance's combustion system, you can help prevent dangerous conditions such as carbon monoxide poisoning and ensure that the appliance operates at peak efficiency.

In the next chapter, we will focus on the detection and repair of gas leaks, a critical aspect of maintaining the safety and integrity of LPG systems.

Chapter 10: Leak Detection and Repair

Leak detection and repair are among the most critical aspects of maintaining the safety and integrity of LPG systems. Even a small gas leak can pose significant risks, including fire, explosion, and exposure to toxic gases like carbon monoxide. As an LPG fitter, it is essential to be skilled in identifying potential leaks and proficient in repairing them quickly and effectively. In this chapter, we will explore the methods used to detect gas leaks, the steps involved in repairing leaks, and best practices for ensuring that the system remains secure and leak-free.

LPG is a highly flammable gas, and its distinctive odor is one of the first indicators of a leak. LPG manufacturers add a chemical called ethyl mercaptan to the gas, giving it a strong, unpleasant smell that is easily recognizable. This odor is often described as similar to rotten eggs, and it serves as an important safety feature, alerting people to the presence of gas even in small quantities. However, relying solely on smell is not sufficient for detecting leaks, especially in outdoor environments where the odor may dissipate or in cases where individuals have a reduced sense of smell. Therefore, additional methods of leak detection are necessary.

One of the most common and effective methods of detecting gas leaks is the use of a **soapy water solution**. This simple technique involves applying a mixture of water and dish soap to the joints, fittings, and connections in the gas system. If there is a leak, the escaping gas will cause bubbles to form in the soapy solution, indicating the location of the leak. This method is particularly useful for detecting leaks in visible and accessible areas, such as around the regulator, hose connections, and appliance fittings.

In addition to the soapy water method, **electronic gas detectors** are commonly used for more precise leak detection. These portable devices are equipped with sensors that can detect even trace amounts of LPG in the air. Gas detectors are particularly useful in situations where visual inspection is difficult, such as in confined spaces or areas where gas may accumulate. When a leak is detected, the detector emits an audible alarm, allowing the fitter to pinpoint the source of the leak quickly and accurately. Gas detectors are an essential tool in any LPG fitter's toolkit and should be regularly calibrated and tested to ensure their accuracy.

Once a leak has been identified, it is critical to take immediate action to repair it. The first step is to **shut off the gas supply** at the source, usually by closing the valve on the LPG cylinder. This prevents further gas from escaping and reduces the risk of fire or explosion while the repair is being carried out. After the gas supply is shut off, the area should be ventilated to disperse any accumulated gas and ensure a safe working environment.

The next step is to **inspect the area** around the leak to determine the cause. Leaks can occur for various reasons, including loose fittings, damaged hoses, corroded pipes, or worn seals. It is important to thoroughly examine all components in the vicinity of the leak, as there may be multiple points of failure. If the leak is due to a loose fitting or connection, it may be possible to stop the leak simply by tightening the fitting. However, care must be taken not to overtighten, as this can damage the threads or cause additional leaks.

If the leak is caused by a **damaged component**, such as a cracked pipe or a worn-out seal, the faulty part must be replaced. This may involve cutting out the damaged section of pipe and installing a new piece, or replacing the defective fitting or seal. When replacing components, it is important to use materials that are compatible with LPG and meet the necessary safety standards. All connections should be securely tightened, and the entire system should be re-tested for leaks after the repair is completed.

In some cases, it may be necessary to use a **sealant** or **pipe joint compound** to ensure a gas-tight connection. These products are applied to the threads of fittings before they are tightened, helping to fill any gaps and prevent gas from escaping. It is important to use only sealants that are specifically designed for use with LPG, as other products may not be effective and could even degrade when exposed to gas. After applying the sealant and making the connection, allow the sealant to cure for the recommended time before pressure-testing the system.

After the repair has been completed, it is essential to **test the entire system** for leaks again. This involves reapplying the soapy water solution to all connections and fittings, as well as using the electronic gas detector to check for any remaining traces of gas. If no leaks are detected, the system can be safely put back into service. It is also important to monitor the area around the repair site for several days afterward to ensure that the leak has been fully resolved and that there are no recurring issues.

In addition to performing repairs, regular **maintenance and inspections** are key to preventing leaks from occurring in the first place. This includes checking all fittings, hoses, and seals for signs of wear or damage, as well as ensuring that the system is properly ventilated and that all components are securely fastened. Regular inspections should be documented, and any issues that are identified should be addressed promptly to prevent them from escalating into more serious problems.

Finally, it is important to **educate your clients** about the signs of a gas leak and the steps they should take if they suspect a leak. Clients should be advised to immediately shut off the gas supply, ventilate the area, and contact a qualified professional to inspect and repair the system. Installing gas detectors in areas where LPG is used is also a valuable safety measure, providing an early warning in the event of a leak.

In conclusion, leak detection and repair are critical responsibilities for any LPG fitter. By using the appropriate methods to identify leaks, taking immediate action to repair them, and maintaining the system regularly, you can ensure the safety and reliability of the LPG installation. Properly addressing leaks not only protects your clients and their property but also helps to prevent potentially life-threatening situations.

In the next chapter, we will discuss the procedures for testing and commissioning LPG systems, ensuring that they are safe, efficient, and ready for use.

Chapter 11: Testing and Commissioning LPG Systems

Testing and commissioning an LPG system are critical steps in ensuring that the system operates safely, efficiently, and in compliance with all relevant standards. These processes involve a series of checks and tests that verify the integrity of the installation, confirm that all components are functioning correctly, and ensure that the system is ready for regular use. In this chapter, we will explore the procedures involved in testing and commissioning LPG systems, along with best practices for documenting the results and obtaining the necessary approvals.

The testing process begins after the installation of the LPG system has been completed and all components have been securely connected. The first test that should be conducted is a **pressure test**. This test is designed to verify the integrity of the piping and fittings by subjecting them to a pressure higher than the normal operating pressure to ensure there are no leaks. The pressure test is typically performed using a manometer or pressure gauge, which is connected to the system to monitor the pressure levels.

To perform the pressure test, start by ensuring that all gas supply valves are closed and that the system is isolated from any connected appliances. Next, introduce air or an inert gas, such as nitrogen, into the system at a pressure that is typically one and a half times the normal operating pressure. The exact pressure required will depend on local codes and standards, so it is important to consult these before beginning the test. Once the system is pressurized, monitor the pressure gauge for a set period, usually around 30 minutes. If the pressure remains stable, this indicates that the system is leak-free. If there is a drop in pressure, it suggests that there is a leak, and further investigation is required to locate and repair it before retesting.

After the pressure test has been successfully completed, the next step is to conduct a **leak test**. While the pressure test checks for the integrity of the system under high pressure, the leak test is performed at normal operating pressure to detect any small leaks that might have been missed. This is done by applying a soapy water solution to all joints, connections, and fittings, as described in previous chapters. If bubbles form, this indicates a leak, which must be repaired before proceeding.

Once the system has passed both the pressure and leak tests, the next step is to **commission** the system by introducing LPG into the piping and appliances. This process involves slowly opening the gas supply valve and allowing gas to fill the system while carefully monitoring the pressure gauge to ensure that it does not exceed the recommended levels. It is important to do this gradually to prevent sudden pressure surges that could damage the system or trigger safety devices.

As the gas is introduced, it is essential to **purge the air** from the system. This is done by opening the gas valves on the appliances to allow the air to escape until a steady flow of gas is detected. The purging process is crucial because any air trapped in the system can cause ignition problems, incomplete combustion, or pressure fluctuations. After purging, the appliances should be ignited one by one to confirm that they are operating correctly and that the gas is being delivered at the correct pressure.

During the commissioning process, it is also important to **test the safety devices** associated with the system. This includes checking the operation of flame failure devices, pressure relief valves, and any other safety mechanisms designed to protect the system and its users. For example, if the system is equipped with an automatic shut-off valve, this should be tested to ensure that it closes properly in the event of a pressure drop or other malfunction. Similarly, if the appliances have thermocouples or flame sensors, these should be checked to confirm that they are functioning correctly.

Another critical aspect of commissioning is verifying that the **ventilation and exhaust systems** are working as intended. This involves checking that all vent pipes are properly connected and free from obstructions, that the exhaust gases are being safely vented to the outside, and that there is adequate air supply for combustion. Proper ventilation is essential for preventing the buildup of harmful gases such as carbon monoxide and ensuring that the system operates efficiently.

Once all tests have been successfully completed and the system is fully operational, the final step in the commissioning process is **documenting the results**. This includes recording the pressure test results, leak test findings, and any adjustments made during the commissioning process. It is also important to note the settings of any regulators, safety devices, or appliances, as well as the dates of all tests and inspections. This documentation serves as a record of the system's compliance with safety standards and provides a reference for future maintenance and inspections.

In some jurisdictions, it may be necessary to obtain **approval from a regulatory authority** before the system can be put into service. This typically involves submitting the test results and documentation to the relevant authority and scheduling an inspection by a certified inspector. The inspector will review the installation, verify that all tests have been conducted correctly, and check that the system complies with local codes and regulations. Once the system has passed the inspection, it can be officially commissioned and put into use.

In conclusion, testing and commissioning an LPG system are essential steps in ensuring that the system operates safely, efficiently, and in compliance with all relevant standards. By following the procedures outlined in this chapter, you can verify the integrity of the system, confirm that all components are functioning correctly, and ensure that the system is ready for regular use. Proper testing and commissioning not only protect the safety of your clients and their property but also help to prevent costly repairs or modifications in the future.

In the next chapter, we will explore troubleshooting techniques for LPG systems, providing guidance on how to diagnose and resolve common problems that may arise during installation or operation.

Chapter 12: Troubleshooting LPG Systems

Even with the most careful installation and diligent maintenance, issues can still arise in LPG systems. When problems occur, it is essential to have a systematic approach to diagnosing and resolving these issues to restore safe and efficient operation. This chapter will guide you through common problems encountered in LPG systems, the symptoms they present, and the steps you can take to troubleshoot and fix them.

The first step in troubleshooting any LPG system is to **observe the symptoms**. Understanding the specific issues being experienced can provide valuable clues as to the underlying cause. Some common symptoms include difficulty igniting appliances, inconsistent flame quality, strange odors, and pressure drops. Each of these symptoms can be indicative of different problems within the system, and identifying the symptom is the first step in determining the appropriate course of action.

Ignition problems are among the most common issues in LPG systems. If an appliance fails to ignite or has difficulty maintaining a flame, the problem could be due to several factors. One of the first things to check is whether the appliance is receiving gas. This can be done by ensuring that the gas supply valve is open and that the pressure at the appliance is within the correct range. If the pressure is too low, it may indicate a problem with the regulator, a blockage in the gas line, or a partially closed valve. On the other hand, if the pressure is too high, it could cause the flame to blow out or be difficult to control, suggesting that the regulator may need adjustment or replacement.

Another common cause of ignition problems is a **blocked burner**. Over time, debris, soot, or corrosion can accumulate in the burner ports, restricting the flow of gas and preventing proper ignition. To resolve this issue, the burner should be removed and thoroughly cleaned. Use a soft brush or compressed air to remove any obstructions from the burner ports, and inspect the burner for signs of damage or excessive wear. If the burner is severely corroded or damaged, it may need to be replaced.

If the burner is clean and the gas supply is functioning correctly, the issue may be related to the **ignition system** itself. Many LPG appliances use electronic igniters, thermocouples, or pilot lights to ignite the gas. If the igniter is not sparking, the thermocouple is not generating a current, or the pilot light is not staying lit, the ignition system should be inspected. Check the wiring and connections to ensure they are secure and free from corrosion. If necessary, replace the igniter, thermocouple, or other faulty components to restore proper operation.

Flame quality is another important indicator of potential problems in an LPG system. A proper LPG flame should be steady and blue, indicating complete combustion. If the flame is yellow, orange, or flickering, it may indicate incomplete combustion, which can be caused by a lack of oxygen, incorrect gas pressure, or a dirty burner. Incomplete combustion not only reduces the efficiency of the appliance but can also lead to the production of harmful carbon monoxide.

To address flame quality issues, start by checking the **air-to-fuel ratio**. Ensure that the appliance is receiving sufficient ventilation and that there are no obstructions in the air intake. Adjust the air shutter on the burner if necessary to allow more air to mix with the gas. Next, check the gas pressure to ensure it is within the recommended range for the appliance. If the pressure is too low, it can cause the flame to be weak and yellow. If the pressure is too high, it can cause the flame to be unstable and noisy.

If the flame quality does not improve after adjusting the air and gas pressure, the problem may be due to a **dirty or damaged burner**. As mentioned earlier, clean the burner thoroughly and inspect it for any signs of damage. Additionally, check the venturi tube, which mixes air with gas before it reaches the burner, for any blockages or debris that could be affecting the flame quality.

Strange odors, particularly the smell of gas, are a serious concern in any LPG system. If you or your client detect the distinctive odor of LPG (often described as smelling like rotten eggs), it is crucial to act immediately. The first step is to shut off the gas supply at the source and ventilate the area. Then, use a gas detector or a soapy water solution to check for leaks at all connections, fittings, and joints. If a leak is detected, it must be repaired before the system can be safely used again.

In some cases, strange odors may not be related to a gas leak but could be caused by **burning debris or dust** on the burner. If the appliance has not been used for some time, dust or other particles may have settled on the burner, causing an unpleasant odor when the appliance is ignited. To resolve this issue, turn off the appliance, allow it to cool, and clean the burner thoroughly before using it again.

Pressure drops within the system can also indicate a problem. If the pressure at the appliances is lower than expected, the first step is to check the regulator to ensure it is functioning correctly and is properly adjusted. If the regulator is working as it should, the issue may be due to a blockage or restriction in the gas line. Inspect the piping for any kinks, bends, or obstructions that could be impeding the flow of gas. Additionally, check the filters in the gas line, if applicable, and clean or replace them as needed.

If the pressure drop occurs suddenly and there are no obvious blockages, it could indicate a **leak** somewhere in the system. In this case, the entire system should be tested for leaks, as described in the previous chapter, and any leaks found must be repaired immediately. Persistent pressure drops may also suggest that the gas cylinder is nearly empty and needs to be replaced.

In some situations, troubleshooting may require a more in-depth investigation using **specialized tools and equipment**. For example, if you suspect that there is a problem with the internal components of an appliance, such as the gas valve or control module, you may need to use a multimeter to test for electrical continuity or a manometer to measure gas pressure more accurately. These tools can help you diagnose more complex issues and determine the best course of action for repairs.

Finally, it is important to keep detailed **records of all troubleshooting efforts**. Documenting the symptoms observed, the steps taken to diagnose the problem, and the repairs performed can be valuable for future reference. It also provides a record of your work that can be shared with your client or used to demonstrate compliance with safety standards.

In conclusion, effective troubleshooting is an essential skill for any LPG fitter. By systematically diagnosing problems, using the appropriate tools and techniques, and addressing issues promptly, you can ensure that LPG systems operate safely and efficiently. Proper troubleshooting not only helps to resolve immediate issues but also prevents potential hazards and costly repairs in the future.

In the next chapter, we will explore advanced LPG fitting techniques, providing guidance on handling more complex installations and specialized equipment.

Chapter 13: Advanced LPG Fitting Techniques

As an LPG fitter gains experience, they may encounter more complex installations that require advanced techniques and specialized knowledge. These advanced projects may involve high-pressure systems, large-scale commercial installations, or the integration of LPG systems with other types of fuel or renewable energy sources. In this chapter, we will explore some of the advanced techniques and considerations that come into play in these more challenging LPG fitting scenarios.

One of the key challenges in advanced LPG fitting is working with **high-pressure systems**. While most residential and small commercial LPG systems operate at relatively low pressures, some industrial applications require higher pressures to deliver sufficient gas flow to large or multiple appliances. High-pressure systems demand more robust materials and components, as well as greater attention to safety procedures.

When working with high-pressure LPG systems, the selection of appropriate **piping and fittings** is crucial. High-pressure systems typically require the use of steel or reinforced piping rather than copper or polyethylene, which may not be able to withstand the increased pressure. The piping should be rated for the specific pressures involved, and all fittings, valves, and regulators must be compatible with high-pressure LPG. It is also essential to ensure that all connections are secure and properly sealed, as even a small leak in a high-pressure system can have severe consequences.

Pressure regulation in high-pressure systems is also more complex. While standard single-stage or two-stage regulators may suffice for low-pressure systems, high-pressure installations often require specialized regulators that can handle the increased pressure while maintaining precise control over the gas flow. In some cases, a series of regulators may be used to gradually step down the pressure from the cylinder to the appliances. This approach ensures that the pressure is reduced in a controlled manner, preventing sudden surges or drops that could damage the system or affect appliance performance.

Advanced LPG fitting projects may also involve **large-scale commercial or industrial installations**. These installations often require the coordination of multiple LPG cylinders or tanks, as well as the integration of LPG with other fuel sources. For example, a commercial kitchen may use LPG for cooking but also have a natural gas line for heating or other applications. In such cases, the LPG system must be carefully designed and installed to ensure that it operates independently from the other fuel sources while still providing the necessary capacity to meet demand.

One of the challenges in large-scale installations is **ensuring a consistent supply of LPG**. In residential settings, a single cylinder or small tank may suffice, but commercial and industrial applications often require larger tanks or multiple cylinders connected in parallel. These systems may also include automatic changeover valves, which switch the gas supply from one cylinder to another when the first cylinder is depleted. Properly sizing the tanks and cylinders, as well as designing the piping system to accommodate the increased flow rates, is essential for ensuring that the LPG supply remains steady and reliable.

Another advanced technique that may be required in large-scale installations is **zoning**. Zoning involves dividing the LPG system into different sections or zones, each of which can be independently controlled. This approach is useful in situations where different areas of a building or facility have varying gas demands or operating schedules. For example, in a large commercial building, the kitchen may require a constant supply of LPG during business hours, while the heating system may only be used during certain times of the day. By zoning the system, you can optimize gas usage and improve overall efficiency.

In some advanced installations, LPG systems may be integrated with **renewable energy sources** such as solar power. For example, a solar thermal system may be used to preheat water, reducing the amount of LPG needed for water heating. Integrating LPG with renewable energy requires careful planning and coordination to ensure that the systems work together seamlessly. This may involve the use of specialized controllers, sensors, and valves that can automatically switch between the LPG and renewable energy sources based on demand and availability.

Remote monitoring and control is another advanced technique that is increasingly being used in LPG systems, particularly in commercial and industrial settings. With remote monitoring, the LPG system can be connected to a network, allowing it to be monitored and controlled from a central location. This is particularly useful for managing large or complex installations where regular manual checks may be impractical. Remote monitoring systems can provide real-time data on gas usage, pressure levels, and system status, as well as alert operators to potential issues such as leaks or low gas levels. In some cases, these systems can even be integrated with building management systems, allowing for centralized control of all the building's energy systems.

Finally, working on advanced LPG fitting projects often requires **collaboration with other trades** and professionals. For example, when installing an LPG system in a new building, you may need to coordinate with electricians, plumbers, and HVAC technicians to ensure that all systems are installed correctly and do not interfere with each other. Effective communication and collaboration are essential for avoiding conflicts and ensuring that the LPG system is integrated smoothly into the overall building infrastructure.

In conclusion, advanced LPG fitting techniques involve working with high-pressure systems, large-scale installations, and the integration of LPG with other fuel sources or renewable energy. These projects require a higher level of expertise, careful planning, and precise execution to ensure that the system operates safely and efficiently. By mastering these advanced techniques, you can take on more challenging and rewarding projects, expanding your skills and opportunities in the LPG fitting industry.

In the next chapter, we will cover exam preparation strategies, offering tips and practice questions to help you succeed in your LPG fitter certification exam.

Chapter 14: Preparing for the LPG Fitter Exam

Preparing for the LPG Fitter certification exam requires a combination of thorough study, practical experience, and effective test-taking strategies. This chapter will guide you through the key steps to ensure you are fully prepared for the exam, including study tips, practice questions, and strategies for managing your time and stress during the test.

The first step in preparing for the exam is to **review the exam content outline** provided by the certifying body. This outline typically lists the topics that will be covered on the exam, along with the weight given to each topic. Understanding the content outline is essential for focusing your study efforts on the areas that will have the most impact on your exam score. While it's important to have a broad understanding of all the topics, you should pay special attention to the areas that carry the most weight.

Next, create a **study plan** that allows you to systematically review all the topics in the exam content outline. Break down the topics into manageable sections and assign specific study times for each section. Consistency is key, so try to study a little bit each day rather than cramming all your study time into a few long sessions. Your study plan should also include time for reviewing your notes, taking practice tests, and addressing any areas where you feel less confident.

One of the most effective ways to reinforce your knowledge is to **practice applying what you've learned** through hands-on experience. If possible, try to get as much practical experience as you can in the weeks leading up to the exam. This could involve working on real-life LPG fitting projects under the supervision of a certified fitter or practicing specific skills, such as pressure testing or leak detection, in a controlled environment. Practical experience not only helps solidify your understanding of the material but also builds your confidence in your ability to perform the tasks required in the field.

In addition to hands-on practice, **practice questions** are an invaluable tool for exam preparation. Practice questions help you become familiar with the format and style of the questions you'll encounter on the exam. They also allow you to test your knowledge and identify any areas where you need further study. Here are some practice questions to help you prepare:

Practice Question 1:

What is the primary function of a pressure regulator in an LPG system?

Answer:

The primary function of a pressure regulator is to reduce the high pressure of the gas in the storage cylinder to a lower, stable pressure suitable for use by the appliances connected to the system.

Practice Question 2:

Why is it important to purge air from an LPG system during commissioning?

Answer:

It is important to purge air from an LPG system to prevent ignition problems, incomplete combustion, and pressure fluctuations. Air in the system can cause the appliances to malfunction and may result in the production of harmful gases like carbon monoxide.

Practice Question 3:

Describe the proper method for detecting a gas leak using a soapy water solution.

Answer:

To detect a gas leak using a soapy water solution, apply the solution to all joints, connections, and fittings in the gas system. If bubbles form in the solution, this indicates the presence of a gas leak, and the connection should be tightened or repaired before re-testing.

Practice Question 4:

What are the signs of incomplete combustion in an LPG appliance?

Answer:

Signs of incomplete combustion in an LPG appliance include a yellow or orange flame (instead of a steady blue flame), soot formation, and the production of carbon monoxide. These symptoms indicate that the air-to-fuel ratio is incorrect, and adjustments may be needed.

Practice Question 5:

When installing an LPG system in a high-pressure application, what material is typically used for the piping?

Answer:

In high-pressure applications, steel or reinforced piping is typically used because it can withstand the increased pressure better than materials like copper or polyethylene.

In addition to reviewing content and answering practice questions, it's important to **develop test-taking strategies** that will help you manage your time and reduce stress on exam day. Here are a few tips:

Read the questions carefully.

Before answering a question, make sure you fully understand what is being asked. Pay attention to keywords and any details that could change the meaning of the question.

Eliminate obviously wrong answers.

If the exam is multiple-choice, try to eliminate any answers that are clearly incorrect. This increases your chances of choosing the correct answer, even if you have to make an educated guess.

Pace yourself.

Keep an eye on the clock and pace yourself so that you have enough time to answer all the questions. If you get stuck on a difficult question, move on and come back to it later if time allows.

Stay calm and focused.

It's natural to feel nervous before an exam, but try to stay calm and focused. Take deep breaths, and remember that you've prepared for this. Confidence in your preparation will help you perform better.

Finally, make sure you are **well-rested and prepared** on the day of the exam. Get a good night's sleep before the exam, eat a healthy meal, and arrive at the testing center with plenty of time to spare. Bring all necessary materials, such as identification, any permitted reference materials, and writing tools, so that you are ready to start the exam without any last-minute stress.

In conclusion, preparing for the LPG Fitter exam requires a combination of focused study, practical experience, and effective test-taking strategies. By following the tips and using the practice questions provided in this chapter, you can approach the exam with confidence and increase your chances of success.

In the next chapter, we will explore career opportunities and professional development in the LPG fitting industry, offering insights into how you can advance your career after achieving certification.

Chapter 15: Career Opportunities and Professional Development

Achieving certification as an LPG Fitter opens up a wide range of career opportunities in the gas fitting industry. Whether you are looking to work for an established company, start your own business, or specialize in a particular niche, there are numerous paths you can take to advance your career. In this chapter, we will explore the various career opportunities available to certified LPG Fitters, discuss the potential for specialization and advancement, and provide guidance on how to continue your professional development.

One of the most common career paths for newly certified LPG Fitters is to **work for an established company** that specializes in gas fitting, plumbing, or HVAC services. These companies often serve both residential and commercial clients, providing a steady stream of work that can help you gain valuable experience in a variety of settings. Working for a company also offers the opportunity to learn from more experienced fitters, develop your skills, and build a professional network. Over time, you may have the chance to advance to a supervisory or management position, where you can oversee teams of technicians and take on more complex projects.

For those with an entrepreneurial spirit, **starting your own gas fitting business** is another viable option. As an independent contractor, you have the freedom to set your own schedule, choose your clients, and build your brand in the industry. Starting your own business allows you to specialize in specific areas of LPG fitting, such as residential installations, commercial systems, or high-pressure applications. However, running your own business also requires strong business acumen, including skills in marketing, customer service, and financial management. If you choose this path, it may be helpful to take additional courses in business management or seek mentorship from other successful entrepreneurs in the field.

Another area of potential specialization is **commercial and industrial LPG systems**. These larger and more complex installations require a higher level of expertise and often involve working with high-pressure systems, large-scale piping networks, and specialized equipment. By focusing on commercial and industrial projects, you can position yourself as an expert in a niche market, which can lead to higher-paying contracts and more challenging work. Specializing in this area may also open up opportunities to work on projects in sectors such as manufacturing, agriculture, or hospitality, where LPG is used extensively.

For those interested in the **renewable energy sector**, there is a growing demand for professionals who can integrate LPG systems with renewable energy sources such as solar or wind power. This type of work involves designing and installing hybrid systems that use LPG as a backup or supplementary fuel source to renewable energy. As the world increasingly focuses on sustainability, having expertise in this area can make you a valuable asset to companies and clients looking to reduce their carbon footprint while maintaining reliable energy supplies.

Continuing education and professional development are essential for staying competitive and advancing in your career as an LPG Fitter. The gas fitting industry is constantly evolving, with new technologies, regulations, and best practices emerging regularly. Staying up-to-date with these changes is crucial for maintaining your certification, expanding your skills, and providing the best possible service to your clients. Consider joining professional organizations such as the National Association of Plumbing-Heating-Cooling Contractors (PHCC) or the American Society of Mechanical Engineers (ASME), which offer access to training programs, certification courses, and industry conferences.

Networking is another important aspect of professional development. Building relationships with other professionals in the industry can lead to new job opportunities, partnerships, and collaborations. Networking can also provide valuable insights into industry trends, client needs, and emerging technologies. Attend industry events, join online forums, and connect with other LPG Fitters through social media platforms like LinkedIn to expand your professional network.

For those interested in **teaching or consulting**, your certification and experience as an LPG Fitter can open doors to roles in education or advisory positions. Technical schools, community colleges, and training programs often seek experienced professionals to teach courses or provide hands-on training to students. Additionally, your expertise can be valuable to businesses, government agencies, or non-profit organizations looking for guidance on LPG projects. Consulting allows you to apply your knowledge in a broader context, often with higher compensation and greater flexibility.

As you progress in your career, you may also consider pursuing **advanced certifications** in related fields, such as HVAC, natural gas systems, or energy management. These additional certifications can enhance your qualifications, broaden your skill set, and increase your marketability to potential employers or clients. Advanced certifications may also qualify you for more specialized or higher-paying roles within the industry.

Finally, it is important to **stay informed about industry trends and innovations**. The gas fitting industry is continuously evolving, with new technologies, materials, and techniques being developed. Staying ahead of these changes can give you a competitive edge and enable you to offer your clients the latest and most efficient solutions. Regularly read industry publications, participate in webinars, and attend trade shows to keep your knowledge current and stay ahead of the curve.

In conclusion, certification as an LPG Fitter is just the beginning of a rewarding and dynamic career. Whether you choose to work for an established company, start your own business, or specialize in a particular area, there are numerous opportunities for growth and advancement. By continuing your education, networking with other professionals, and staying informed about industry trends, you can build a successful and fulfilling career in the LPG fitting industry.

This concludes **"Conquer™ the LPG Fitter Exam: Your Guide to Certification in Liquified Petroleum Gas Fitting."** The detailed information, practical insights, and strategies provided in this book should equip you with the knowledge and confidence you need to pass your certification exam and pursue a successful career in the LPG fitting industry. Thank you for your commitment to safety and excellence in your work, and best of luck in your future endeavors!

Printed in Great Britain
by Amazon